First World War
and Army of Occupation
War Diary
France, Belgium and Germany

59 DIVISION
Headquarters, Branches and Services
Adjutant and Quarter-Master General
1 January 1916 - 31 August 1916

WO95/3012/1

The Naval & Military Press Ltd
www.nmarchive.com
Published in association with The National Archives

Published by

The Naval & Military Press Ltd

Unit 10 Ridgewood Industrial Park,

Uckfield, East Sussex,

TN22 5QE England

Tel: +44 (0) 1825 749494

www.naval-military-press.com

www.nmarchive.com

Contents

Document type	Place/Title	Date From	Date To
Heading	WO95/3012/1 59 Div HQ. Branches Services Adjutant Quarter Master General Jan 1916-Aug 1916		
Heading	59th (North Midland) Division A & Q. Branch 1916 Jan-1916 Aug		
War Diary	St Albans	01/01/1916	28/04/1916
War Diary	Kingstown	28/04/1916	31/04/1916
War Diary	Dublin	01/05/1916	28/07/1916
War Diary	Curragh	02/08/1916	31/08/1916

WO 95/3012/1

59 DIV

HQ BRANCHES & SERVICES

ADJUTANT & QUARTERMASTER GENERAL

Jan 1916 – Aug 1916

59TH (NORTH MIDLAND) DIVISION

A & Q. BRANCH

1916 JAN — 1916 AUG

January 1916

WAR DIARY
or
~~INTELLIGENCE SUMMARY.~~
(Erase heading not required.)

59 N M Division
A & Q Branch

Army Form C. 2118.

Instructions regarding War Diaries and Intelligence Summaries are contained in F. S. Regs., Part II. and the Staff Manual respectively. Title pages will be prepared in manuscript.

Place	Date	Hour	Summary of Events and Information	Remarks and references to Appendices
St ALBANS	1.1.16		Epidemic of scabies again broke out in the Division	LAMW
	7.1.16		Major E.L.L. BRADBRIDGE appointed AA & QMG & takes over duty from Col J.A. FEARON & to be tempy Lt Col whilst so employed	LAMW LAMW
	8.1.16		Brigadier General BLACKADER DSO ADC takes over command of 177th Infty Bde from Col G M JACKSON TD	LAMW LAMW
	12.1.16		2/1 NM Field Ambulance move by march route from WATFORD to HARPENDEN	LAMW
	"		2/2 NM Field Ambulance move by march route from HARPENDEN to WATFORD	LAMW
	13.1.16		The Division comes under the command of GOC 3rd Army	LAMW
	14.1.16		Inspection of Mobile Vety Section by Col DWYER	LAMW
	15.1.16		S/c COOPER & Cpl MATTHEWS MM [illegible] came ex-ALDERSHOT	LAMW
	18.1.16		Capt RWS STANTON Reserve of Officers appointed DAA & QMG	LAMW
	19.1.16		2/4 Leicester Regt moved by march route from HARPENDEN to LUTON	LAMW
	21.1.16		RAMC exercises (450 casualties to be fed & warmed)	LAMW
	22.1.16		All remounts were malleined. No reactions reported	LAMW
	22.1.16		DDVS C Force visited Division re lice	

1377 Wt. W10791/1773 500,000 1/15 D. D. & L. A.D.S.S./Forms/C. 2118.

January 1916.

59 N M Division (A & Q Branch)

Army Form C. 2118.

Instructions regarding War Diaries and Intelligence Summaries are contained in F. S. Regs., Part II. and the Staff Manual respectively. Title pages will be prepared in manuscript.

WAR DIARY
or
~~INTELLIGENCE~~ SUMMARY.

(Erase heading not required.)

Place	Date	Hour	Summary of Events and Information	Remarks and references to Appendices
St ALBANS	27.1.16		The Field Ambulance was inspected by DMS Central Force	[illegible]
	28.1.16		2/4 How^r Bde RFA rearmed with 4.5" guns & wagons.	[illegible]
	29.1.16		12 Infty Units received 100 Rifles SMLE each	[illegible]
	30.1.16		Army Dental officer reported for duty.	[illegible]
			Two 15 pr BLC Guns & equipt transferred to FRESHWATER Redoubt.	[illegible]
	31.1.16		100 Horses of RA proceeded to Southminster	[illegible]
	31.1.16		2/3 N M Bde RFA moved by rail from BOXMOOR to SOUTHMINSTER	[illegible]

W W Bradbridge
Lt.-Colonel.
A.A. & Q.M.G. 59th (North Midland) Division.

1577 Wt. W10791/1773 500,000 1/15 D. D. & L. A.D.S.S./Forms/C. 2118.

Instructions regarding War Diaries and Intelligence Summaries are contained in F. S. Regs., Part II. and the Staff Manual respectively. Title pages will be prepared in manuscript.

WAR DIARY
or
INTELLIGENCE SUMMARY.
(Erase heading not required.)

Army Form C. 2118. 1

A2Q 5W HQ
59th Division

Place	Date	Hour	Summary of Events and Information	Remarks and references to Appendices
ST ALBANS	1-2-16		Rev A. JUDD C.F. 4th Class reported his arrival	RWSS
	2-2-16		Rev A CHAPLIN C.F 4th Class reported his arrival	RWSS
	" "		Rev Archdeacon L KLUGH C.F & Rev G.S MORRELL C.F struck off strength of Division	RWSS
	" "		G.O.C 3rd ARMY visited the Division & inspected Headquarters Offices	RWSS
	4-2-16		Rev E.K QUICK C.F struck off strength of Division	RWSS
	"		Rev T.D. THOMAS A.C.F reported his arrival.	RWSS
	6-2-16		Rev A.G BAGSHAW A.C.F reported his arrival	RWSS
	10-2-16		Col L GRAHAM R.A is appointed C.RA & takes over the duties in relief of Colonel	RWSS
			A.H.C PHILLPOTTS R.A from 7th inst.	RWSS
	" "		Rev J. GOODACRE C.F. reported his arrival	RWSS
	12-2-16		No 4 Company A.S.C moved from WATFORD to ST ALBANS being relieved by No 2 Company A.S.C from ST ALBANS	RWSS
	14-2-16		Major General A.E. SANDBACH C.B. D.S.O takes over command of the Division from Major General R.N.R READE C.B	RWSS
	16-2-16		Colonel L.R. CARLETON D.S.O relinquishes appointment of G.S.O I of the Division & takes over command of 176th Infantry Brigade in relief of Colonel H. CHANDOS POLE-GELL.	RWSS

[signature] Lt.-Colonel.
A.A. & Q.M.G. 59th (North Midland) Division.

T2134. Wt. W708—776. 500000. 4/15. Sir J. C. & S.

Instructions regarding War Diaries and Intelligence Summaries are contained in F. S. Regs., Part II. and the Staff Manual respectively. Title pages will be prepared in manuscript.

WAR DIARY
or
INTELLIGENCE SUMMARY.
(Erase heading not required.)

A & Q. Div H.Q.
5-9 Division

Army Form C. 2118. 2.

Place	Date	Hour	Summary of Events and Information	Remarks and references to Appendices
St ALBANS	16-2-16		Major T.A WALSH SOMERSET L.I takes over duties of Brigade Major 176th Infantry Bde vice CAPT C.O. LANGLEY.	Rws
			CAPT C.O LANGLEY takes over duties of STAFF CAPTAIN 176th Infantry Bde vice Captain A.E WILEY	Rws
			Lieut Hon H.N. DOUGLAS-PENNANT is taken on the strength as A.D.C to Major General SANDBACH vice Lieut C.L.C CLARKE.	Rws
	17-2-16		Major G.B.G WOOD The Lancashire Fusiliers assumes duty as Bde Major 177th Infty Bde vice Lt Col C.R STAVELEY & is taken on the strength of the Division	Rws
	18-2-16		Lt Col. R. St G. GORTON R.G.A assumes duty as G.S.O I & is taken on the strength of the division.	Rws
	19-2-16		Lt Col MAXWELL A.D.V.S Central Force visits Artillery Brigades.	Rws
	20-2-16		Following Units attached to the Division 2/2 COUNTY OF LONDON YEOMANRY 1/1 HANTS HEAVY BATTERY. 2/1 HANTS HEAVY BATTERY	
	23-2-16		Division comes under W.E Part VIII.	Rws
	25-2-16		Designation of Companies of Divisional Train changed to 513. 514. 515 & 516 Companies A.S.C. respectively	Rws

T2134. Wt. W708—776. 500000. 4/15. Sir J. C. & S.

[signature]
A.A. & Q.M.G. 53th (North Midland) Division.

Instructions regarding War Diaries and Intelligence Summaries are contained in F. S. Regs., Part II. and the Staff Manual respectively. Title pages will be prepared in manuscript.

WAR DIARY
or
INTELLIGENCE SUMMARY.
(Erase heading not required.)

Army Form C. 2118.

Place	Date	Hour	Summary of Events and Information	Remarks and references to Appendices
ST ALBANS	25-2-16		Lt Col L HAYWOOD R.A.M.C (T) having been appointed to command a Hospital vacates the appointment of D.A.D.MS & is struck off the strength of the Division	RWB
	26-2-16		1/3rd N.M. FIELD COY. R.E proceeded to BRIGHTLINGSEA for a course of instruction.	RWB
	28-2-16		Following Officers proceeded overseas for duty & return on 3-3-16 COL A.V. CLARKE. A.D.M.S. Lt Col E.U BRADBRIDGE A.A & Q.M.G.	RWB
	"		A.D.V.S Central Force inspected horses of WESSEX R.G.A prior to their departure.	RWB
	29-2-16		Emergency entrainment practiced. G.O.C III Army visited ST ALBANS & inspected units of 176th Infantry Bde - parading for this practice.	RWB

E U Bradbridge Lt.-Colonel.
A.A. & Q.M.G. 59th (North Midland) Division.

Instructions regarding War Diaries and Intelligence Summaries are contained in F. S. Regs., Part II. and the Staff Manual respectively. Title pages will be prepared in manuscript.

WAR DIARY
or
INTELLIGENCE SUMMARY.
(Erase heading not required.)

ADVS.

Army Form C. 2118.

Duplicate of Monthly War Diary for inclusion with H.Q.

Place	Date	Hour	Summary of Events and Information	Remarks and references to Appendices
St. Albans.	3/2/16.		Attended board on death of horses which died 23/1/16 under suspicious circumstances.	
,,	5/2/16.		Reported to A.A.G 2329 V ., re poor shoeing in Division.	
,,	[illegible]/2/16.		Visited No 4 Coy ABC. Watford. Reported unsatisfactory condition of horses to C/C ASC.	

1577 Wt. W10791/1773 500,000 1/15 D. D. & L. A.D.S.S./Forms/C. 2118

1.3.16. Major C W W McLean DSO appointed for duty as Bde Major 59 S.M. Div artillery vice Maj H C Bryan [illegible]

1.3.16. Major W F McAllister Hennings RAMC(T) appointed for duty as DADMS 59th S.M. Div vice Lt Col. Hyam [illegible]

1.3.16. Rev W O Leadbitter CF transferred to Division & struck off strength of Division

2.3.16. Lt J A McLaughlin AVC(TF) transferred to 61st S M Division & struck off strength of Division

7.3.16. (5) Lt Col Stock DADR & 2 Mules inspection horses of Division

5.3.16. Major Gen E T Dickson Inspector of Infantry inspected the battalion of the Division also on 7th 9th & 10th (also on 8th 9th 10th 11th)

10.3.16. Lt Gen Sir A Codrington KCB GOC III Army inspected remounts of the Division

10.3.16. Major H W D Stokes ASC takes over duties of DAQMG vice Major F S Thornton

10.3.16. 2/2 County of London Yeomanry struck off strength of the Division

13.3.16. Major G B Roberts takes over duties as CRE vice Lt Col W E Harrison

14.3.16. Capt R W S Stanton DAA & QMG appointed President of the Central Lunacy Committee vice Major F S Thornton

21.3.16. 50 Men from 3 Line N M Div Cyclist Coy joined 59 S M Div Cyclist Coy & taken on strength of Division

25.3.16. 1/3 NM Field Coy RE moved from Brightlingsea to Bentley

59 S M Div Signal Coy moved from Ampthill to ~~Bentley~~ to Kelvedon

28.3.16. "C" Squadron Northumberland Hussars. 6 officers 136 other ranks under command of Major the Hon Jasper Ridley ~~[illegible]~~ arrived & taken on strength of Division as Divisional Cavalry

A War Diary. April 1916

[S]T ALBANS. 3rd 4th ADVS inspected the horses of the Division
5th Division comes on War Establishments PART VII
18th Brigadier-General E J R Peel DSO RA takes over command of the Divisional RA from Col L. Graham CMG who proceeds to assume another command
11 Advance Parties of Division proceeded to CODFORD SALISBURY PLAIN.
20 Rev G. KENDALL CF UNITED BOARD joined for duty & is posted to 177th INFANTRY BDE
22 Advance Parties returned from CODFORD.
24 Division ordered to hold itself in readiness to move at short notice
25 176th & 178th Infantry Bdes with Sections of Field Ambulances entrained for IRELAND.
2/2 Field Company RE & 2/1st F A Brigade entrained.
26 3/1 Field Company entrained & remainder of Division ordered to proceed.
27 Division commenced embarking for KINGSTOWN at LIVERPOOL
28 Division commenced to disembark at Kingstown
Base Supply Depot established at KINGSTOWN.
Capt A BILLSON 2/4th LEICESTER Regt appointed TOWN COMMANDANT with local rank of MAJOR

Divisional Head Quarters established next-door to the MARINE HOTEL

KINGSTOWN 28th Divisional Ordnance Depot opened at PAVILION KINGSTOWN

Lieut Colonel GOLDSMITH R.A.M.C reported temporarily for duty as A.D.M.S.
& 3 Medical Officers temporarily attached for duty.

28th All Civilians & soldiers not on duty ordered to be in their houses by 7.30pm

29th Divisional Head Quarters moves to the MASONIC SCHOOL at BALLSBRIDGE, the 2/1st
N M [illegible] Infantry Bde less 1 Battalion, & Divisional Troops proceeded
to BALLSBRIDGE & were accommodated in the ROYAL SOCIETY'S SHOW GROUNDS.
The Divisional Casualty Clearing Station under command of CAPTAIN HEATH
disembarked & were stationed at KINGSTOWN
Lt Col A H C DENT R.A.M.C (T) appointed A.D.M.S of the Division
A Despatch Rider Letter Service between DIVISIONAL HEADQUARTERS &
KINGSTOWN established
CAPT L A F WEIGALL 5th Lincoln Regt appointed acting APM at BALLSBRIDGE

30th 117 Rebels surrendered to 5th Bn Lincoln Regt & were handed over to APM
& were accommodated under guard in SHOW GROUND

31st Divisional Head Quarters moved to 23 & 46 N. CIRCULAR ROAD DUBLIN

31st

The following casualties were reported in the Division up to 31st

2/7 Sherwood Foresters Killed Captain & Adjutant F.C DIETRICHSEN. LIEUT F.C PERRY. 2/Lieut W.V. ~~HAWKEN~~ Other ranks 5. Wounded Lt Col C FANE D.S.O. MAJOR H HANSON, Capt F.G. HICKLING. CAPT F PRAGNELL 2/Lieut J.E HARTSHORN 2/Lieut W.F. FISHER 2/Lieut F.M. LAMB. & CAPT R.A CHARLTON Other ranks 60 = 24

Missing 29.

2/6 Sherwood Foresters Killed other ranks 1. Wounded other ranks 5

~~2/8 Sherwood Foresters~~ Killed Lieut H.C DAFFEN, (Died of wounds) 2/Lieut M.B. BROWNE. Other ranks 7. Wounded Captain A.H QUIBELL, CAPT & ADJUTANT A.B LESLIE MELVILLE CAPTAIN F.G. CURSHAM. LIEUT C.P ELLIOT. 2/LIEUT W.H CURTIS 2/LIEUT J.E BROAD Other ranks 53. Missing 13

2/5 S. Stafford Regiment Killed (died of wounds) other ranks 1. Wounded 6.

2/6 S Stafford Regiment. Killed other ranks 11. (died of wounds) 3 Wounded. Captain P.S BAYLISS, CAPT DENNING, CAPT J SHEPPARD 2/Lieut G.H HALLIWELL. Other ranks 27 Missing 1.

2/5 LEICESTER Regt. Other ranks wounded 1.
59th Div SIGNAL Coy. Injured 2/Lieut TISSINGTON. Wounded other ranks 1
Total Killed Officers 5 Other ranks 30. Wounded Officers 19. Other ranks
153 Missing 38.

205

Instructions regarding War Diaries and Intelligence Summaries are contained in F. S. Regs., Part II. and the Staff Manual respectively. Title Pages will be prepared in manuscript.

Army Form C. 2118

WAR DIARY
or
INTELLIGENCE SUMMARY
(Erase heading not required.)

A & Q

MAY 1916.

Place	Date	Hour	Summary of Events and Information	Remarks and references to Appendices
DUBLIN	1st		Divisional Head Quarters moved from BALLSBRIDGE to 46 N. CIRCULAR ROAD DUBLIN	Ross
"	2nd		Detachment consisting of 7 armoured motor cars with 9 officers & 37 other ranks is attached to the Division & accommodated in ROYAL BARRACKS under command of CAPT REEVE	Ross
"	3rd		Major T.B. THORNE Middlesex Regt assumed command of 2/6 N. STAFFS REGT.	Ross
			Field Post Office established at Divisional Head Quarters.	
	"		Capt H.M. WHITEHEAD appointed Acting A.P.M. at DIVISIONAL HD QTRS during MAJOR RHODES's absence on duty at KINGSTOWN	
	4th		Following rebels executed under arrangements made by the Division. EDWARD DALY WILLIAM PEARSE JOSEPH PLUNKETT & MICHAEL O'HAUREHAN	
			The following were executed on 3rd May P.H. PEARSE THOMAS MACDONAGH & THOMAS CLARKE.	
	"		The Dublin Corporation placed the IVEAGH BATHS at the disposal of the Division	
	5th		Divisional Postal Section 1 N.C.O. & 10 men reported for duty	
			All officers & details attached to the division during the Rebellion ordered to join their units.	
			The following rebel was executed - JOHN McBRIDE	
	8th		The following rebels were executed. EDMUND KENT. MICHAEL MALLON. J.J. HEUSTON. CORNELIUS COLBERT.	
	9th		Major H.C. MAITLAND-MAKGILL-CRICHTON D.S.O Royal Scots Fusiliers reported for duty as G.S.O. 2 vice Lt Colonel C.F. HEYWORTH-SAVAGE R.G.O.	

(1875) Wt. W393/826 - 1,000,000 4/15 J.B.C. & A. A.D.S.S./Forms/C. 2118.

Instructions regarding War Diaries and Intelligence Summaries are contained in F. S. Regs., Part II. and the Staff Manual respectively. Title Pages will be prepared in manuscript.

WAR DIARY
or
INTELLIGENCE SUMMARY
(Erase heading not required.)

Army Form C. 2118

Place	Date	Hour	Summary of Events and Information	Remarks and references to Appendices
~~DUBLIN~~	~~10th~~		~~Appointment of Divisional Remount Officer abolished.~~	
	"		Standing Court of Enquiry under BRIG GEN. BLACKADER. appointed to enquire into certain charges against the troops.	
	12th		Major H. R. GOODMAN. R. IRISH RIFLES appointed Brigade Major 178th Infantry Bde vice CAPT. A. N. LEE 7th Sherwood Foresters	
			Following rebels executed.	
			JAMES CONOLLY & JOHN McDERMOTT	
			52 Other ranks from 27th Provisional Battalion & 48 from 26th Provisional Battalion posted to the Division.	
	15th		The following numbers are allotted to Artillery Brigades of the Division	
			295. 296. 297 & 298.	
	"		Two Battalions S. STAFFS REGT proceeded to STRAFFAN for Musketry	
	16th		D.R.L.S between KINGSTOWN & DUBLIN discontinued & D.R.L.S between STRAFFAN & DUBLIN established.	
	"		Standing Court of Enquiry under Colonel E. S. K MACONCHY appointed.	
	20th		Official time of Division put on one hour in accordance with the Time Alteration Act.	
	22nd		Divisional Artillery commenced Artillery Practice at GLEN. IMAIL	
	23rd		Divisional Head Quarters moved to the CHIEF SECRETARYS LODGE PHOENIX PARK	
			16 other ranks posted to the Division from the 29th Provisional Battalion	

1875 Wt. W593/826 1,000,000 4/15 J.B.C. & A. A.D.S.S./Forms/C. 2118.

Instructions regarding War Diaries and Intelligence Summaries are contained in F. S. Regs., Part II. and the Staff Manual respectively. Title Pages will be prepared in manuscript.

WAR DIARY
or
INTELLIGENCE SUMMARY
(Erase heading not required.)

Army Form C. 2118

Place	Date	Hour	Summary of Events and Information	Remarks and references to Appendices
DUBLIN	25th		Major A. R. HENCHLEY R.A.M.C assumes command of the Divisional Casualty Clearing Station.	
	29th		D.R.L.S between GLEN IMAIL / DUBLIN arranged to leave daily at 8 am / return same day.	
			Divisional Pigeon Service established between STRAFFAN / DUBLIN.	

1875 Wt. W593/826 1,000,000 4/15 J.B.C. & A. A.D.S.S./Forms/C. 2118.

Instructions regarding War Diaries and Intelligence Summaries are contained in F. S. Regs., Part II. and the Staff Manual respectively. Title Pages will be prepared in manuscript.

WAR DIARY or INTELLIGENCE SUMMARY

A & Q

JUNE 1916

(Erase heading not required.)

Army Form C. 2118

Place	Date	Hour	Summary of Events and Information	Remarks and references to Appendices
DUBLIN	1-6-16		Capt R L BENSON 9th Lancers reported for duty as G.S.O. 3 vice Capt R. RAY who proceeded to join 3rd KINGS OWN Regt at PLYMOUTH	
			1 Officer & 43 OR reported for duty with 2/6 S. STAFFS Regt.	
	3-6-16		25 O.R reported for duty with 2/6 N. STAFFS Regt.	
			9 O.R reported for duty with 2/5 S. STAFFS Regt.	
	7-6-16		All officers of the Division went into Mourning for one week on occasion of the death of the late F M Rt Hon Earl Kitchener of Khartoum.	JUNE
	8-6-16		59th Divisional Casualty Clearing Station moved from KINGSTOWN to PHOENIX PARK	
			Authority to discharge recruits under KR 392(iiic) & (iii c.c) delegated to Divisional & Brigade Commanders.	
	13-6-16		Col E. S. W. MACHONCHY C.B. C.I.E. D.S.O. Commanding 176th Infantry Bde to be (temp) BRIGADIER GENERAL	
	16-6-16		2/6 N. STAFFS Regt relieves detachments of 2/5 N STAFFS Regt in DUBLIN	
			2/5 N. STAFFS concentrates in PHOENIX PARK.	
	19-6-16		102 other ranks arrived for duty with 59th Divisional Train.	
	20-6-16		Major T HAZLERIGG A.S.C. assumed duty as O.C 59th Divisional Train vice Lt Col READING	
			Capt V.D.R. CONLAN A.S.C assumed duty as S.S.O of the Division vice Maj JONES	

Instructions regarding War Diaries and Intelligence Summaries are contained in F. S. Regs., Part II. and the Staff Manual respectively. Title Pages will be prepared in manuscript.

WAR DIARY
or
INTELLIGENCE SUMMARY
(Erase heading not required.)

Army Form C. 2118

Place	Date	Hour	Summary of Events and Information	Remarks and references to Appendices
DUBLIN	22-6-16		2/5 N. STAFFS Regt marched to STRAFFAN	
			2/5 S. STAFFS Regt marched from STRAFFAN to PHOENIX PARK.	
			Lt Col C MAC I RITCHIE assumes command of 296th Bde R.F.A & troops PHOENIX PARK	
	23-6-16		2/5 S STAFFS Regt relieved detachment of 2/6 N STAFFS Regt in DUBLIN	
			2/6 N STAFFS concentrated in PHOENIX PARK.	
	24-6-16		2/6 N. STAFFS Regt marched to STRAFFAN	
			2/6 S. STAFFS. marched from ~~PHOENIX~~ STRAFFAN to PHOENIX PARK	
	25-6-16		Major J. Stuart WORTLEY R of O joined for duty with 2/5 S. STAFFS Regt.	
			Lt Col H TAYLOR 2/6 S STAFFS Regt assumes command of troops PHOENIX PARK.	
	28-6-16		Lt Col BRIDGES assumed command of 295th Bde R.F.A.	
			Inspector of Remounts Irish Command inspects horses of Divisional Head Qrs 59th Signal Co. 59th Cyclist Co. 2/5 & 2/6 S. STAFFS Regt. Head Quarters Company A.S.C	
			Brigadier General C H L JAMES CB assumes command of 177th Infty Bde vice Brigadier General C. J. BLACKADER D.S.O. A.D.C. who proceeds for duty overseas.	
	29-6-16		Lectures on precautions for combatting Gas attacks.	
	30-6-16			

Instructions regarding War Diaries and Intelligence Summaries are contained in F. S. Regs., Part II. and the Staff Manual respectively. Title Pages will be prepared in manuscript.

Army Form C. 2118

WAR DIARY
or
INTELLIGENCE SUMMARY A & Q JULY 1916
(Erase heading not required.)

Place	Date	Hour	Summary of Events and Information	Remarks and references to Appendices
DUBLIN	1st		Captain T H LINCOLN R.E.T. assumes command of the 59th Divisional Signal Company vice Major C C HURST	
	"		Owing to shortage of supplies, daily allowance of potatoes purchased out of the $5\frac{1}{2}$d messing allowance limited to ½ lb per man	
	3rd		An additional THRUSH DISENFECTOR authorised for issue to the division.	
	4th		Brigadier General A.W. ROPER C.B. Inspector R.E. inspected 59th Divisional Signal Company.	
	5th		Capt A.E PERRY KNOX-GORE. K.O. YORKSHIRE L.I. appointed Brigade Major 176th Infantry Bde vice Capt A.C ADAIR Scots Fusiliers.	
			Rev DELAFIELD C.F. United Board & Rev MURPHY C.F. R.C proceeded to join 31st Stationary Hospital Aldershot before proceeding Overseas.	
	6th		Orders received for reorganization of DIVISIONAL ARTILLERY. Howitzer Brigade being split up & one battery allotted to each of 3 F.A Bdes. Remaining (298th) Brigade to consist of 3 four gun batteries.	
			Lt Col de SATGE remains in command of 298th Bde as now constituted	
	8th		Detachment 178th Infantry Bde proceeded to Aldershot for Trench Mortar Course.	
	11th		Inspector of Remounts Irish Command inspected horses of 178th Infy Bde at Curragh.	

1875 Wt. W593/826 1,000,000 4/15 J.B.C. & A. A.D.S.S./Forms/C. 2118.

Instructions regarding War Diaries and Intelligence Summaries are contained in F. S. Regs., Part II. and the Staff Manual respectively. Title Pages will be prepared in manuscript.

WAR DIARY
or
INTELLIGENCE SUMMARY
(Erase heading not required.)

Army Form C. 2118

A + Q. JULY 1916

Place	Date	Hour	Summary of Events and Information	Remarks and references to Appendices
DUBLIN	12th		Redistribution of Commands in Ireland approved by Army Council	Rws
			MIDLANDS + CONNAUGHT DISTRICT to be under the Command of Major General A.E. SANDBACH C.B. D.S.O with Head Quarters at CURRAGH	Rws
			One intelligence officer (extra) to be attached to Divisional Staff	
	15th		Detachment 177th Infantry Brigade proceeded to Aldershot for Trench Mortar Course.	Rws
			Abolition of Brigade Ammunition Columns decided on by War Office	Rws
	17th		Lt L.G.A. CUST 3rd Home Counties Bde R.F.A appointed A.D.C to CRA	Rws
	20th		Rev N. KNOCK Wesleyan Chaplain reported for duty & posted to 178th Infty Bde.	
	22nd		W.O rule that N.C.Os & men of Division may be sent on Harvest Leave the numbers so permitted to be included in the 10% allowed away at one time	Rws
	26th		Divisional Troops start moving to Curragh.	Rws
			H.Qs & No 513 Company 59th Divisional Train - move to A.S.C Lines	
			H.Qs & No 1 Section Divisional Signal Company to No 4 Camp.	Rws
			C Squadron Northumberland Hussars to K Lines	
	28th		Divisional Head Quarters move to Curragh.	Rws
			Head Quarters Offices to District Lodge	

1875 Wt. W593/826 1,000,000 4/15 J.B.C. & A. A.D.S.S./Forms/C. 2118.

Army Form C. 2118

Instructions regarding War Diaries and Intelligence Summaries are contained in F. S. Regs., Part II. and the Staff Manual respectively. Title Pages will be prepared in manuscript.

WAR DIARY
or
INTELLIGENCE SUMMARY July

(Erase heading not required.)

Place	Date	Hour	Summary of Events and Information	Remarks and references to Appendices
Dublin	28th		Divisional Cyclist Company moves from Phoenix Park to BERESFORD BKS. Divisional Commander & A Mess move from Chief Secretary's Lodge Phoenix Park to BALLYFARE HOUSE CURRAGH	RW

1875 Wt. W593/826 1,000,000 4/15 J.B.C. & A. A.D.S.S./Forms/C. 2118.

Instructions regarding War Diaries and Intelligence Summaries are contained in F. S. Regs., Part II. and the Staff Manual respectively. Title Pages will be prepared in manuscript.

WAR DIARY
or
INTELLIGENCE SUMMARY
(Erase heading not required.)

AUGUST 1916
A + Q

Army Form C. 2118

Place	Date	Hour	Summary of Events and Information	Remarks and references to Appendices
CURRAGH	2nd		Capt (temp Major) G T SPEIR appointed temporary Lieut Colonel & assumes command of the 2/5 S. Staffs Regt vice Lt Col H TAYLOR who is posted to the T.F. Reserve	RM
"	4th		1/2 Battalion 2/5 Sherwood Foresters marched from COOLMONEY CAMP to CURRAGH & are accommodated in HARE PARK HUTMENTS	RM
	5th		1/2 Battalion 2/6 Sherwood Foresters marched from CURRAGH to COOLMONEY CAMP	RM
			59th Divisional Cyclist Company rejoined at the CURRAGH from ORANMORE	RM
	7th		Party of 500 other ranks arrived at STRAFFAN from 65th Division for musketry	RM
	8th		4/6th Sherwood Foresters arrived at Curragh from ATHLONE	RM
	9th		Details of Echelon A DIVISIONAL AMMUNITION COLUMN arrived at KILDARE from LUTON	RM
			Major C A STIDSTON assumes command of 3rd Field Ambulance vice Lt Col POCKETT	RM
	10th		Capt J. DODDS A O D assumes the duties of D.A.D.O.S vice CAPT. G F A WEBSTER	RM
	11th		Headqrs 176th Infantry Bde & 1 Battalion proceeded from STRAFFAN to PHOENIX Park DUBLIN	RM
	15th		Field Marshal Commander in Chief Home Forces inspected 176th Bde at PHOENIX Park Dublin	RM
	16th		Inspection of 178th Bde, Divisional RA & Divisional Troops at the Curragh by the Field Marshal C in C Home Forces	RM
			Field Post office closed	
	17th		Inspection 177th Infty Bde by Field Marshal C in C Home Forces at FERMOY	RM

1875 Wt. W593/826 1,000,000 4/15 J.B.C. & A. A.D.S.S./Forms/C. 2118.

Instructions regarding War Diaries and Intelligence Summaries are contained in F. S. Regs., Part II. and the Staff Manual respectively. Title Pages will be prepared in manuscript.

WAR DIARY
or
INTELLIGENCE SUMMARY
(Erase heading not required.)

Army Form C. 2118

Place	Date	Hour	Summary of Events and Information	Remarks and references to Appendices
Curragh	23rd		Lt Col (temp Brigadier General) E J R PEEL is struck off the strength of the Division on posting to 58th Division	
	28th		Issue of satchels for antigas helmets up to 10 per cent of strength authorised	
	29th		Brigadier General G.M. GLOSTER C.M.G. assumes command of 176th Infty Bde vice Brigadier General L.A CARLETON	
			59th Div Casualty clearing station moved from DUBLIN to BRAY for employment in Princess Patricia's Hospital.	
	31st		Capt G.E. TALLENTS D.S.O Lancashire Fusiliers assumes duty as Brigade Major 177th Infty Brigade.	

1875 Wt. W593/826 1,000,000 4/15 J.B.C. & A. A.D.S.S./Forms/C. 2118.

www.ingramcontent.com/pod-product-compliance
Lightning Source LLC
Chambersburg PA
CBHW081507160426
43193CB00014B/2614